WORLD IN PERIL

RIVERS
UNDER THREAT

PAUL MASON

Heinemann
LIBRARY

www.heinemannlibrary.co.uk
Visit our website to find out more information about Heinemann Library books.

To order:

☎ Phone +44 (0) 1865 888066

🖹 Fax +44 (0) 1865 314091

🖳 Visit www.heinemannlibrary.co.uk

Edited by Louise Galpine and Rachel Howells
Designed by Richard Parker and Manhattan Design
Picture research by Hannah Taylor and Rebecca Sodergren
Production by Alison Parsons
Originated by Dot Gradations Ltd.
Printed in China by Leo Paper Products Ltd.

ISBN 978 0 431020 57 0 (hardback)
13 12 11 10 09
10 9 8 7 6 5 4 3 2 1

British Library Cataloguing in Publication Data
Mason, Paul
Rivers under threat. – (World in peril)
577.6'4

A full catalogue record for this book is available from the British Library.

Acknowledgements
We would like to thank the following for permission to reproduce photographs: Alamy Images pp. **13** (Eye Ubiquitous), **17** (Bettina Strenske), **19** (Boats/ Tina Manley); Corbis pp. **4** (image100), **25** (Ed Kashi); Creatas p. **14**; FLPA p. **20** (Sunset); Getty Images pp. **6** and **16** (Hulton Archive), **8** (Bryce Duffy), **21** (National Geographic/ Richard S. Durrance); NHPA p. **18** (Mark Carwardine); Panos pp. **12** (Mark Henley), **23** (Georg Gerster); Photolibrary pp. **22** (Corbis), **26** (Cusp/ Jason Hosking), **27** (Roy Morsch); Reuters pp. **9** (Jitendra Prakesh), **15** (Aly Song); Rex Features p. **24** (Sabah Arar); Science Photo Library pp. **10** and **11** (NASA); Skyscan.co.uk p. **7** (K. Whitcombe).

Cover photograph of polluted river, reproduced with permission of Still Pictures (Lineair/ Ron Giling).

We would like to thank Michael Mastrandrea for his invaluable help in the preparation of this book.

Every effort has been made to contact copyright holders of material reproduced in this book. Any omissions will be rectified in subsequent printings if notice is given to the publishers.

All the Internet addresses (URLs) given in this book were valid at the time of going to press. However, due to the dynamic nature of the Internet, some addresses may have changed, or sites may have changed or ceased to exist since publication. While the author and Publishers regret any inconvenience this may cause readers, no responsibility for any such changes can be accepted by either the author or the Publishers.

Contents

Some words are printed in bold, **like this**. You can find out what they mean by looking in the glossary.

What's so good about rivers?

Rivers bring life to the land. All living things need water to survive, and without rivers the **water cycle** would not work. Rainfall fills rivers, streams, and lakes with water. The water **flows** down rivers to the sea. From the sea it is drawn up into the sky, forming clouds. Later, rain falls from the clouds. The whole cycle starts again.

Not all of a river's water makes it to the sea. Trees and plants use water to grow. Animals use water for drinking. Humans have depended on rivers for thousands of years. We use them for drinking, to water crops, and for **industry**. Rivers also provide transport for goods and people.

Today, many rivers are under threat from human activity. We take too much water from them, and pump **pollution** back in. Some rivers are drying up before they reach the sea. Others are so dirty that their water is now dangerous to drink.

How much water can we each have?

This photograph shows the town of Perth, Scotland, around 1935. The River Tay **flows** through Perth. For hundreds of years the Tay provided the townspeople with water.

In 1925 there were about two billion people in the world. This was the largest population the world had ever had. People were using more water than ever before. They used the extra water to grow food, cook, and wash themselves.

How much bigger does Perth look in this photograph than the
one on page 6? Like Perth, the world's population had grown
much bigger by 2000. It had trebled, to six billion people.

By 2025, it is predicted that the world's population will have risen
to 7.5 billion. Yet the amount of fresh water in the world never
changes. As the population grows, each person's share of the
water decreases.

Can river water affect human health?

Does this water look clean enough for a swim? In the past, many people got their water for washing, drinking, and watering their crops straight from rivers, lakes, and wells.

People who lived beside rivers would sometimes put their rubbish into them, too. This included **sewage**. You might think this was not very nice for the people living downstream! In fact, the sewage was usually broken down in the water and became harmless.

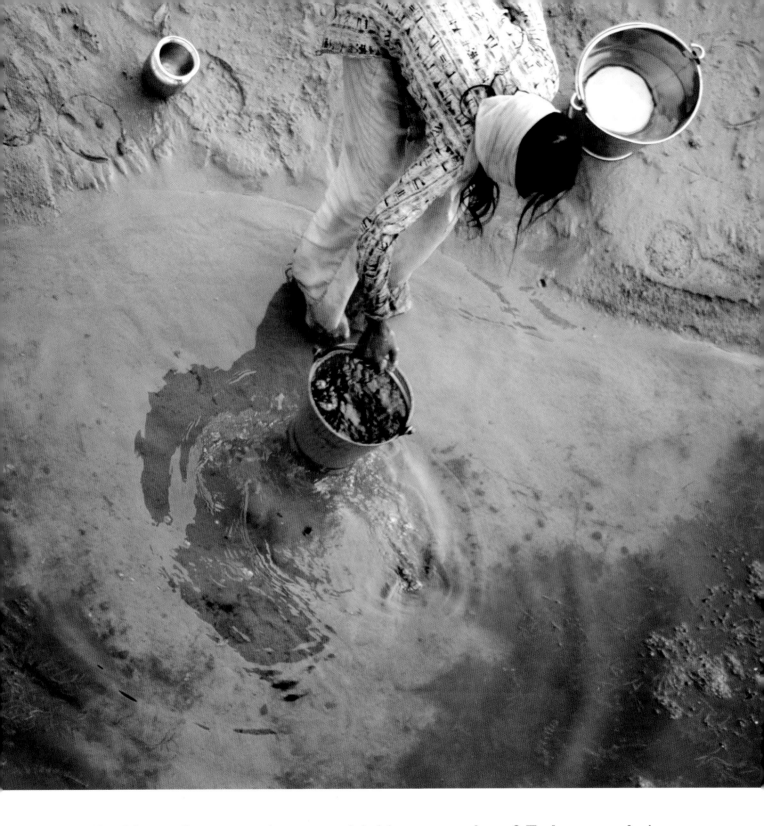

Would you fancy getting your drinking water here? Today, people in wealthy countries have clean water **piped** to their homes. But many people in poor countries still get their water from the same rivers they dump waste into.

Because there are so many more people today than in the past, the rivers cannot cope with the amount of waste. It stays in the water, causing sickness and disease.

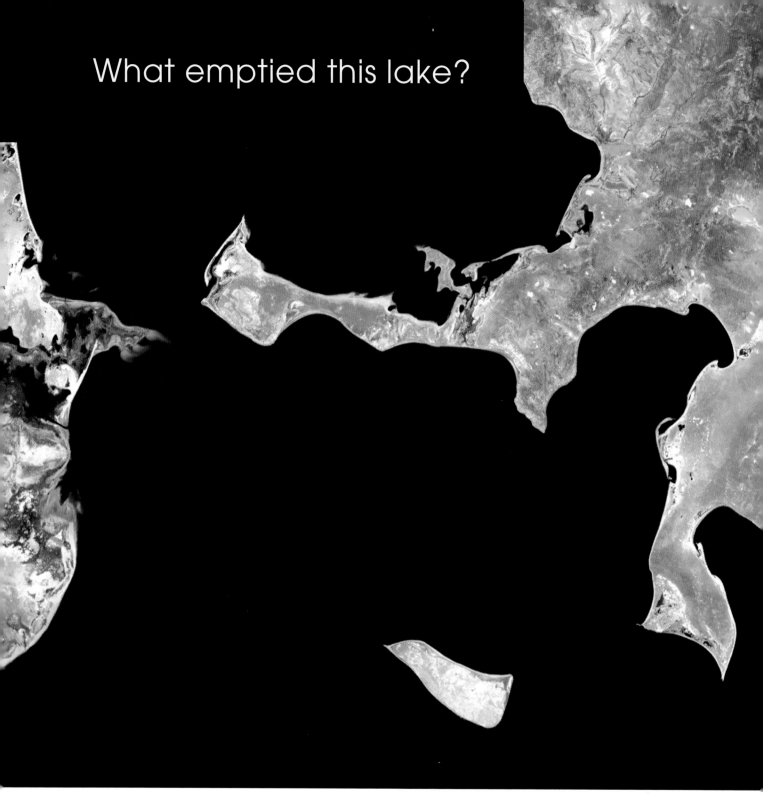

What emptied this lake?

These photographs show the Aral Sea, between Uzbekistan and Kazakhstan. It was once the fourth-largest inland sea in the world, with busy **ports** and a big fishing **industry**.

During the 1960s, the Aral Sea began to shrink. The black area on the left-hand photograph shows the sea in 1973. The rivers that fed it brought less water to the sea each year. The reason was that **upstream**, water was being taken from the river for **irrigation**.

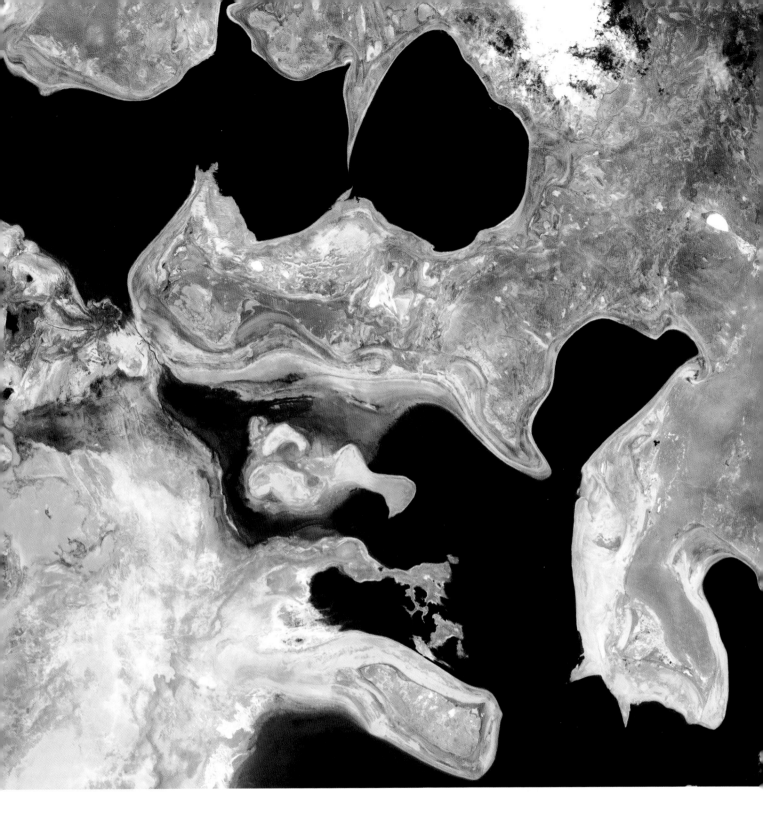

By the time the right-hand photograph was taken in 2000, the Aral Sea had shrunk to a quarter of its original size. The fishing boats were left stranded on dry land. The water had become saltier, killing many of the plants and fish.

Today, many other water stores are in danger of drying up. One of the main reasons is the amount of water we use for farming. Farming uses up 7 litres out of every 10 (1.8 gallons of every 2.6).

Why does this river sometimes run dry?

This is the Huang He, or Yellow River, in China. It is one of Asia's biggest rivers. Even so, during China's dry season the Huang He slows to a trickle. Some years, the river's **mouth** is completely dry, and it does not even reach the sea.

This happens because so much water is taken from the river for farming. Five times as much is taken today as was taken in 1950.

Would you recognize this as the same river? The Chinese government wants the Huang He to **flow** like this all the time. The river would then provide plenty of water for farming.

The government has come up with a plan to **divert** some of the water from other rivers into the Huang He. Canals would be built between the rivers. When finished, the canals will be able to carry up to 44.8 billion m^3 (11,800 billion gallons) of water each year.

Imagine going fishing and hooking such a huge animal! Rivers such as this one are home to a complicated **food chain**. The plants provide shelter for all sorts of animals, from snails to fish. Tiny river creatures such as shrimps are food for small fish. The smaller fish are **prey** for bigger fish. Ducks, rodents, and other animals live near the banks. They rely on the river for food and water.

This river running through farmland is choked with weeds. Farming has caused the problem. The farmer has used **fertilizer** to make the crops grow faster and bigger. When it rains, some of the fertilizer is washed into the river. It helps weeds and **algae** grow quickly. They suck all the oxygen out of the water. With no oxygen to breathe, the other river life dies out.

What gave this river new life?

This is the River Thames in 1971. At this time, the Thames was badly **polluted**. Many other rivers also became badly polluted from the 1950s onwards. Factories near the river poured pollution into the water. The fish and other river life were killed.

Waste is still poured straight into many rivers. The Yangtze River in China, for example, has roughly 40 million tonnes of **industrial** waste and raw **sewage** poured into it – every day!

In 1971, who would have guessed that by 2008, people would be catching fish in the Thames once more?

Like many big-city rivers in wealthy countries, the Thames has been cleaned up. Rubbish and pollution have been cleared away. The authorities watch carefully to make sure there is no new pollution. As the rivers become cleaner, wildlife returns to the river.

Why are there no more of these dolphins?

The baiji is a freshwater dolphin from the Yangtze River in China. These dolphins were once worshipped in China, but during the 1950s people began to hunt them. The numbers of baiji began to fall, and by the early 2000s there were few left.

Many **rare** animals make their homes along the Yangtze. Another is the Siberian crane, which could soon become **extinct**.

The Three Gorges Dam across the Yangtze River was finished in 2006. The **dam** flooded a huge area of land. The rising waters drove many animals, and millions of people, from their homes. The lake flooded the winter resting grounds of the Siberian cranes, which is why they may soon die out completely. The baiji dolphins could no longer move up and down the river, and now seem to be extinct.

What stopped the snake river salmon?

These salmon are heading **upriver** in the Pacific Northwest, USA. Once there, they will **spawn** by laying eggs. When the eggs hatch the young fish will make their way back downriver to the sea.

For thousands of years, the Native American people of the region have relied on the salmon for food. Many fishermen and wildlife also visit the river, hoping to catch salmon as they journey **upstream**.

Would you be able to swim past this **dam** on the Snake River in Washington, USA? Most salmon can't! Dams block the river, making it harder for the salmon to get to and from their spawning places.

The dams do have "fish ladders" for the salmon to leap up, but they do not work well. Spawning places that once saw hundreds of thousands of fish are now only reached by a few.

What dried out the wetlands?

Wetlands such as this one in Australia do an important job for rivers. Imagine them as a giant sponge. The sponge soaks up **impurities**, such as grains of dirt, in the water. It also makes sure the water does not **flow** too quickly.

Wetlands are also home to many different plants and animals. Some of them are very **rare**, and only live in one or two places.

Can you believe that these camels are crossing what was once a wetland? Between 1900 and 2000, half the world's wetland areas disappeared. Sometimes **dams** and **irrigation** schemes **upstream** meant that less water reached the wetlands, and they dried up. Other wetlands were drained deliberately, to make land for farming or even house building. Either way, the wetland animals and plants lost their homes. Without the wetlands to control water flow, floods became more common.

How can rivers cause wars?

This woman in Baghdad, Iraq, is doing her washing in the Tigris River. In dry parts of the world such as the **Middle East**, water is a precious **resource**. There is barely enough for people's needs. If the rivers fail for some reason, it is a disaster.

In places like this, fighting over water is common. Almost always, the problem starts because one person thinks another has taken more than their fair share of water.

This Turkish **dam** is holding back the waters of the Euphrates.
The rivers Tigris and Euphrates **flow** from Turkey into Syria and
Iraq. Turkey's dams make it possible to keep the water for their own
use. Less water flows into other countries. As a result, Syria and
Iraq have accused Turkey of causing water shortages in their
countries. How would you feel about this, if you were a Turkish or
Iraqi farmer?

Are there ways to help the rivers?

The best hope for rivers and lakes in the future is for humans to use less water. Of every ten buckets we take, seven are used in farming. We can all help to save water by buying food that does not require lots of water to be produced.

Cows like this one eat grain, which is produced by using a lot of water. This means it takes over four times more water to produce beef than chicken. Eating chicken instead of beef saves water!

How else can you save water? There are lots of things people can do at home. You can water the garden with a watering can instead of a hose. Water-saving showerheads cut the amount of water used for washing. Cleaning bikes or cars with a bucket and sponge instead of a hose saves water, too.

By working together, and only using the water we need, we may be able to keep rivers **flowing** for years to come.

WHAT DID YOU FIND OUT ABOUT RIVERS?

Why are rivers important?
Tip: think about the life that rivers give to humans, plants, animals, and insects, and the **industries** that are helped by rivers. Page 5 gives a good summary, but also read over the chapters throughout the book for specific examples.

Why should we worry about rivers?
Hint: the photographs on pages 15, 19–20, 21, and 23 might give you some ideas about the plants and animals that depend on rivers, as well as the kinds of landscapes rivers bring water to.

Does farming help rivers, or harm them? Explain why.
Tip: the first-ever farms grew up next to rivers tens of thousands of years ago. They needed water from rivers to grow crops. But farming is very different today. Pages 10–11, 15, and 23 will give you some ideas about how farming has affected rivers.

How are rivers linked to our factories and businesses?
Hint: have a look at the photographs on pages 16–17, 19, and 21 to get some ideas.

How do we affect rivers from far away?
Tip: finding answers to this question might not be easy. Most people know that turning on a tap might affect our rivers and lakes. But how might less obvious things, such as turning on a light, or flushing the toilet, affect them?

Would you like to live next to a sewage farm? Why or why not?
Hint: in some countries, **sewage** waste is pumped into rivers. If it does not go there, it has to be treated in a sewage farm to make it safe. But most people refuse to allow a sewage farm near their homes. Would you be one of them?

How do rivers change our lives?
Tip: make a list of the positive ways in which rivers affect us. It
should detail how rivers help us live comfortable and well-fed lives.
Look at the photographs on pages 7–8, 17, 25–26, and 27 to get
some ideas.

What would life be like if we left rivers as they are?
Hint: how would your life have to change if we left rivers as they
exist naturally, and no longer took water from them for farming,
dammed them for energy, or used them to wash away our waste?
Would you notice a difference?

What are some things you can do to help rivers survive?
Tip: your answer might include things like how much water you
use, what happens to your waste water, what you eat, and how
much energy you use.

Glossary

algae tiny plants that grow in water or moist ground

dam man-made barrier, designed to hold back water

divert change the path of

extinct no longer in existence. If all the world's raccoons died out, for example, raccoons would have become extinct.

fertilizer chemical added to soil to help plants grow. Chemicals washed off the soil and into rivers can affect the plants and animals that live there.

flow move smoothly in one direction

food chain group of plants and animals that are linked together because each one further up the chain depends on the ones below it for food

impurity anything that stops something being pure. In water, impurities could include bits of earth or rock, rotting material, or pollution.

industry business or activity that produces goods for sale

irrigation use of extra water to help crops grow

Middle East area of land surrounded by the eastern Mediterranean Sea, Black Sea, and Arabian Sea

mouth place where a river reaches the sea

piped moved in a pipe

pollution dirt that harms the environment

port place where ships can load and unload their goods or passengers

prey animal or animals that are hunted by others as food

rare unusual, not found very often

resource useful raw material

sewage human toilet waste mixed with water

spawn produce eggs or young

upriver towards the high ground where a river began, rather than towards the sea

upstream against the flow of water in a river. Since rivers flow downhill, upstream is always uphill.

water cycle constant process where water falls as rain, finds its way to the sea, moves back up into the sky, and falls as rain again

Find out more

Books

Mapping Earthforms: Rivers, Catherine Chambers and Nicholas Lapthorn (Heinemann Library, 2007)

Rivers and Lakes, Richard Beatty (Raintree, 2003)

River Explorer, Greg Pyers (Raintree, 2004)

Rivers Through Time, various (Heinemann Library, 2005)

Websites

www.panda.org/about_wwf/what_we_do/freshwater/about_freshwater/rivers

An excellent page from the World Wide Fund For Nature. Clicking on the links takes you to information about 18 of the world's biggest, most important rivers. Click on the river's name to find out more. The "Problems" and "Solutions" tabs also take you to interesting information.

http://assets.panda.org/downloads/worldstop10riversatriskfinalmarch13.pdf

Links to a PDF document from the World Wide Fund for Nature, giving details of the 10 most at-risk rivers in the world: the Salween-Nu, Danube, La Plata, Rio Grande-Rio Bravo, Ganges, Indus, Nile, Murray-Darling, Mekong-Lancang, and Yangtze.

Index